B1

Renfrewshire
Council

The library is always open at
renfrewshirelibraries.co.uk

Visit now for
homework help
and free
eBooks.

SKOOBS

We are the Skoobs and we love the library

Phone: 0300 300 1188
Email: libraries@renfrewshire.gov.uk

A nurse timeline

ca. 3000-100 BCE

In ancient Egypt, India and Greece, priests and (mostly) male servants treat patients in temples.

ca. 500-1500 CE

Nuns (and some monks) care for the dying in hospitals close to churches. Islamic charities run hospitals in Muslim lands.

ca. 1850-1880

Clara Barton, Dorothea Dix and other reformers campaign for better health care and nurse training in the United States.

ca. 300 BCE-300 CE

Male nurses look after Roman soldiers injured in battle.

ca. 1600-1900

Rich people, religious groups and charities in Europe and America pay for local private hospitals. Nuns and charity-workers visit the sick and dying.

Early 1900s

Governments pass laws controlling nurse registration.

1854-1860

Florence Nightingale reforms nursing in UK army hospitals, and sets up a pioneer nurse training school.

1960

The first university degree course in nursing is offered, in Scotland.

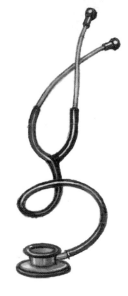

1914-1918 and 1939-1945

Thousands of nurses care for troops in two world wars. They win great respect and admiration.

1861-1865

Untrained women volunteer as nurses on both sides in the American Civil War.

2015

There are over 20 million trained nurses working worldwide. At least 75 percent are women.

The Nightingale Pledge

In 1893, in Detroit, USA, pioneer nurse educator Lystra Gretter suggested that newly trained nurses should make a solemn promise to uphold the highest possible standards of nursing care. Gretter called this promise 'The Nightingale Pledge', in honour of Florence Nightingale. Many nurses, all round the world, still make a similar promise at their graduation ceremonies today.

Here is Gretter's Nightingale Pledge, in modern words:

'In front of God and all the people gathered here today I promise to live honestly and decently, and faithfully to practise my profession as a nurse.

I will not do anything wicked or hurtful to myself or to others, and I will not give patients any harmful medicines.

'I will do all I can to uphold and improve high standards of nursing care. I will keep all information about my patients and their families strictly confidential.

I will work loyally in a team with all other health care professionals. It is my mission to bring health, and so I dedicate myself to working devotedly for human welfare.'

Florence Nightingale is also honoured every year on International Nurses Day. It is celebrated worldwide on 12th May. Why was that date chosen? It was Florence Nightingale's birthday!

Author:

Fiona Macdonald studied history at Cambridge University, England, and at the University of East Anglia. She has taught in schools, adult education and universities, and is the author of numerous books for children on historical topics.

Artist:

David Antram was born in Brighton, England, in 1958. He studied at Eastbourne College of Art and then worked in advertising for 15 years before becoming a full-time artist. He has illustrated many children's non-fiction books.

Series creator:

David Salariya was born in Dundee, Scotland. He has illustrated a wide range of books and has created and designed many new series for publishers in the UK and overseas. David established The Salariya Book Company in 1989. He lives in Brighton with his wife, illustrator Shirley Willis, and their son Jonathan.

Editor: Jacqueline Ford

Editorial Assistant: Mark Williams

PAPER FROM
SUSTAINABLE
FORESTS

Published in Great Britain in MMXVII by
Book House, an imprint of
The Salariya Book Company Ltd
25 Marlborough Place, Brighton BN1 1UB
www.salariya.com
www.book-house.co.uk
ISBN: 978-1-911242-30-7

1 3 5 7 9 8 6 4 2

A CIP catalogue record for this book is available from the British Library.

Printed and bound in China.

Visit our website at **www.salariya.com** for **free** electronic versions of:
You Wouldn't Want to be an Egyptian Mummy!
You Wouldn't Want to be a Roman Gladiator!
You Wouldn't Want to be a Polar Explorer!
You Wouldn't Want to sail on a 19th-Century Whaling Ship!

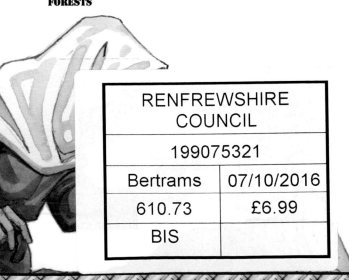

Very important!

The text and pictures in this book are for interest and information only. THEY ARE NOT MEDICAL ADVICE. If you are worried about your health, you should see a doctor, nurse, or other health professional.

You Wouldn't Want to Live Without™
Nurses!

Written by
Fiona Macdonald

Illustrated by
David Antram

Series created by
David Salariya

BOOK HOUSE
a SALARIYA *imprint*

Contents

Introduction

Usually you're healthy and full of energy. But just the other day, you had a nasty accident. You fell off your bike, bumped your head, and broke your arm and your leg! Now you're in hospital, but you're getting better quickly and will soon go home. As you lie in your hospital bed, you think about the nurses who are looking after you. They are so kind, so patient, so caring. They've done such a lot to help you. Imagine if you didn't have someone to look after you when you were poorly. Nurses do such an important job around the world, and help so many people to feel better every day. You really wouldn't want to live without nurses!

Call the nurse!

Have you ever been taken ill at school, or fallen over and hurt yourself while playing? Then the school nurse probably looked after you. She cleaned your cuts, checked that no bones were broken, and said a few kindly words to comfort you. Like all other nurses around the world, your school nurse has been trained to examine her patients, assess (judge) their medical needs, and provide the correct advice or treatment. Every day, school nurses help students in so many different ways.

LICE AREN'T NICE!
Lice feed on human blood and their bites are itchy. Nurses search hair so that lice can be found, removed, and stopped from spreading to and infecting other people.

ONWARDS AND UPWARDS.
School nurses keep careful records of your height and weight to check that you are growing in a healthy way.

10

The school nurse can also teach you how to care for your teeth so that they stay clean, healthy and strong. Remember to brush your teeth at least twice a day, and always at bedtime.

EAT WELL, STAY WELL.
Good food helps bodies grow and minds develop. The school nurse can tell you what's best to eat to help you reach your full potential.

DAILY DOSE.
If you have a health condition and have to take pills or use an inhaler, the school nurse can help you make sure that you're getting the right amount of medicine.

11

A caring career

A school nurse is just one kind of nursing professional. There are many, many others. Today, nurses can choose to train for over 200 special duties. But wherever nurses work and whatever nurses do, they all have one thing in common: they have made caring their career. Caring is not only being kind – though it includes that, of course. Nurses also need patience, toughness, cheerfulness, a real interest in other people, and a willingness to cope with messy, yucky tasks.

The six 'C's

Nurses often say that they need six special personal qualities to do their job well. Each one begins with the letter C. The best nurses have them all!

Care

Compassion

Do you have what it takes to be a nurse? Try this test and see! Are you:

Hard-working? ☐
Unselfish? ☐
Patient with others? ☐
Trustworthy? ☐
Thoughtful? ☐
Sympathetic? ☐
Intelligent? ☐
A good team player? ☐

Competence

Communication

Courage

Commitment

Nursed at home

owadays, we expect trained nurses to look after us when we fall ill. However, until recently, most people had to manage without professional nursing care. For thousands of years, mothers, wives and daughters looked after poorly loved ones at home. In the past, people thought that caring was a natural female instinct, as well as a woman's duty. But of course not all women were born with nursing skills! Until the 19th century, most family carers had no training, but relied on advice from older, more experienced, women. That could sometimes be dangerous!

SICK IN BED? Until around 1800, the local wise woman might have offered you one of her home remedies made from herbs – perhaps with added magic!

WORTH THE MONEY? Until the 20th century, if you were old or ill but wealthy, you could hire a private nurse. She'd have been pleasant and polite, but wouldn't have known much about medicine.

POOR, HOME ALONE, and needing care? Before around 1850, a cheap nurse would have watched by your bedside – but might have been dirty, lazy and a gossip.

EXPECTING A BABY? After around 600 BCE, you could hire a fashionable new man midwife. He would have had more training than a woman, but less expcrience.

How it works

In the past, in remote areas, there might have been no doctors or nurses for hundreds of miles. So medicine chests were kept stocked with remedies for common illnesses.

I told you not to eat so much!

MOTHER CARE.
Our modern word 'nurse' comes from the Latin word *nutrix*, which is over 2,000 years old. It means 'person who feeds babies and cares for them' – like a human or animal mother.

Care not cure

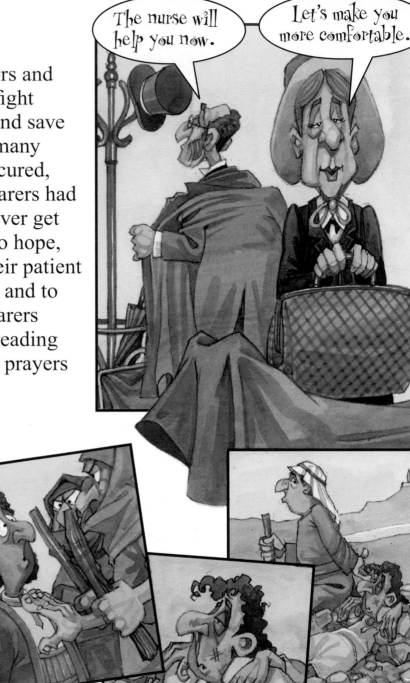

The nurse will help you now.

Let's make you more comfortable.

Today, we admire doctors and nurses as heroes who fight disease, heal injuries and save lives. But in the past, many illnesses could not be cured, and nurses or family carers had to look after people who would never get better. If a doctor said there was no hope, it was still a carer's job to keep their patient clean, warm, fed, free from pain – and to help them go to the toilet. Some carers offered spiritual comfort, too, by reading holy books to patients, and saying prayers with them.

The Good Samaritan

In Christian countries, the Bible story of the Good Samaritan was very popular. It told how a stranger cared for a badly injured man, even though he came from a different community. It contained a powerful message: we should all help people in trouble, whoever they may be.

Attacked...

...left to die...

...robbed!

Oh no! The doctor can't cure him!

A stranger approaches...

...helps the poor victim...

...takes him to safety...

...and pays for his care.

17

Houses of healing

Today, if we are really ill, we go to hospital. But in the past, there were not many hospitals – and they were not healthy places to be. Until around 1850, most hospitals were run by charities or religious organisations. They were often crowded, and they were always smelly and full of germs (bacteria and viruses). Sick people were sent there to keep them away from healthy men and women. Or they went to hospital to die, if there was no one to care for them at home.

STAY AWAY. In the Middle Ages, to avoid catching diseases, people would send a sick person to a 'pest house', far out of town.

MAGIC OR MEDICINE? In ancient Egypt or Greece, ill people could go to a temple, where priests would ask the gods to cure them. The priests might also try to heal someone with medicines, simple surgery, or magic amulets, like the Eye of Horus, below. Their male servants helped them, like nurses.

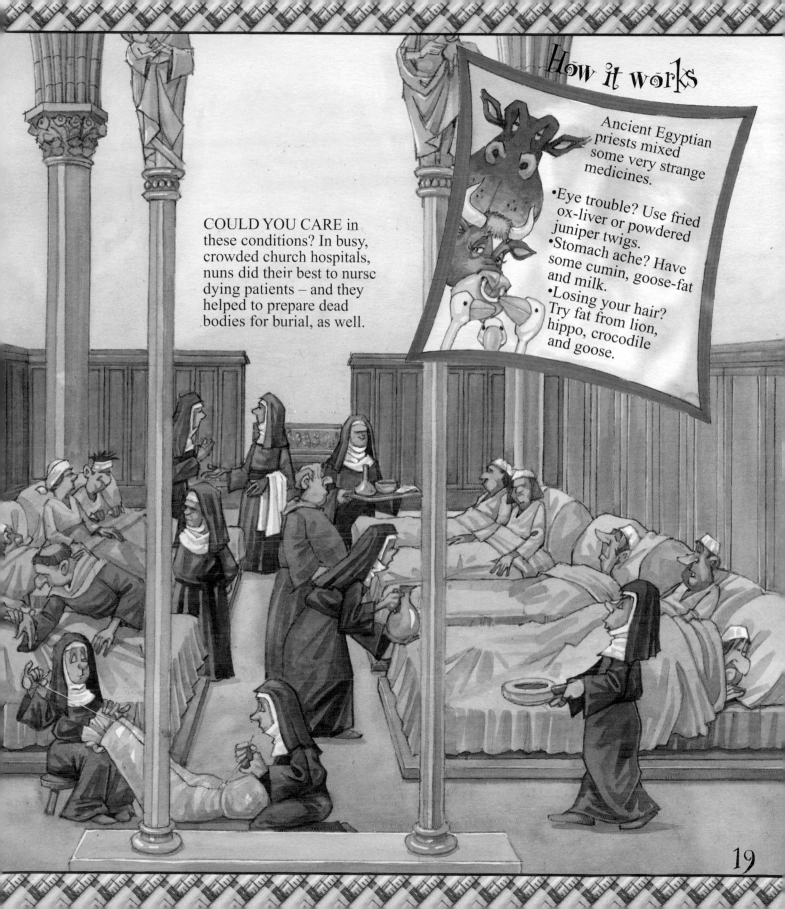

How it works

Ancient Egyptian priests mixed some very strange medicines.

- Eye trouble? Use fried ox-liver or powdered juniper twigs.
- Stomach ache? Have some cumin, goose-fat and milk.
- Losing your hair? Try fat from lion, hippo, crocodile and goose.

COULD YOU CARE in these conditions? In busy, crowded church hospitals, nuns did their best to nurse dying patients – and they helped to prepare dead bodies for burial, as well.

The new nurses

Nowadays, we know that germs cause disease, and that keeping clean is an important part of staying healthy. But until around 1850, nobody understood why dirt could be dangerous. Doctors and nurses often wore dirty clothes, and visitors described horrific conditions in hospitals. Not only were they filthy, they also lacked good food, clean water, soap, bandages, medicines and proper nursing care. There was a public outcry that 'something must be done!'. Brave, determined reformers took up the challenge, training new, professional nurses and keeping hospitals superclean.

Look, listen and learn!

THE LADY WITH THE LAMP. That's what they called Florence Nightingale (1820–1910). In 1854, she was sent to a British army hospital in Turkey to treat British soldiers of the Crimean War. Appalled by the dirt (and rats!) she worked tirelessly to improve cleanliness and patient care. In 1860, she set up the world's first nonreligious nurse training school. Her work made her a national heroine, and created a new public respect for trained, skilled nurses.

TO TRAIN TO BE a new nurse, you'd learn anatomy (body structure) and physiology (how the body works), and about medicines, hygiene and hospital routine.

Beginning in 1903 (in the US) and 1919 (in the UK), nurses had to be properly trained and registered with nursing associations. Before those dates, almost anyone could call themselves a nurse.

Clara Barton (1821–1912)

Dorothea Dix (1802–1887)

BATTLEFIELD ANGELS. Around 5,000 untrained women volunteered to care for wounded soldiers during the American Civil War (1851–1865). They were led by Clara Barton (who also founded the American Red Cross) and health-care campaigner and prison reformer Dorothea Dix. Leaders and volunteers bravely did their best, but the war showed that the USA urgently needed trained nurses. The first US nurse training school opened in New York City in 1871.

Observation and communication

As well as keeping us clean and comfortable, nurses listen to our worries and explain our medical treatments to us in ways we can understand. They sympathise with grieving family members when patients die, and speak up for patients who are unable to put their thoughts and feelings into words. Doctors also rely on nurses to observe patients' vital signs, such as temperature, breathing and heart rate, and keep accurate records of them. That is a big responsibility!

HEALING HANDS. A nurse's gentle touch will soothe you, but she's also feeling for signs of illness, such as clamminess or shivering.

He's getting better! Do you want to tell him, or shall I?

TOO HOT? TOO COLD?
The nurse will take your temperature. If it's too high, too low, or keeps changing, that could be a sign of illness.

BREATHE IN… AND OUT…
Are you coughing or wheezing? Pains in your chest? The nurse will use a stethoscope to check your heart and lungs.

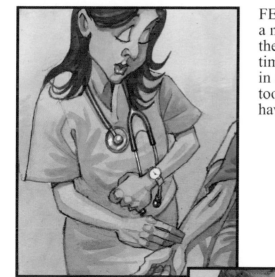

FEEL THE BEAT. When a nurse takes your pulse, they count the number of times that your heart beats in a minute. Too many or too few may mean you have health problems.

In intensive care units each nurse monitors and looks after just one or two patients. In general wards, where lives are not in danger, each nurse might have from five to eight patients to observe and care for.

PUMP IT UP. When we are well, our hearts pump blood at a steady, even pressure. But this changes when we are ill, so nurses check it carefully.

TLC (TENDER LOVING CARE)—AND MUCH MORE. In addition to observing their patients, kind, caring nurses do a great deal to calm, comfort and encourage them. They also 'speak up' for patients, communicating their needs and fears and worries, when patients are too old, young or ill to express themselves.

WRITE IT DOWN. Records of vital signs show how ill a patient is, or how well they are recovering. Florence Nightingale was the first to make nurses record patient information. It is still very useful for medical staff today.

23

Think clearly, act quickly, keep calm

Wars, earthquakes, floods, famines, epidemics, transport accidents and terrorist attacks all bring tragedy to our world. Who do we turn to for help in these disasters? Very often, it's a nurse. Along with local volunteers, nurses are usually the first on the scene in any emergency. Hundreds of lives may depend on their actions. They are highly-trained professionals, and many are amazing heroes. But, even so, their work is extremely stressful and demanding. Could you cope?

DISASTER ZONE. Some nurses are specially trained to help people after natural disasters, such as major earthquakes. They must adapt to their surroundings and think on their feet.

It's not easy, but I've been trained for this!

You can do it!

Using a library or the internet, look up some of the countries where nurses from the Red Cross and the Red Crescent are working, and find out how they have helped the people in those areas.

This is what we've practised for!

LIFE SAVERS. From small beginnings in 1863, the International Red Cross and Red Crescent Movement has grown to become the largest humanitarian (caring) organisation in the world. Today, it has almost 100 million staff and volunteers. They help any human in need, anywhere.

SURVIVING STRESSFUL SITUATIONS.

If you're a nurse and you can't cope, you can't help others. So:

1. Look after yourself, as well as your patients.
2. Eat well and exercise.
3. Find time to rest and relax.
4. Speak up about any problems.
5. Share your worries and fears.
6. Get training for new or difficult tasks.
7. Practise for emergencies.
8. Learn to work well in a team.
9. Don't be afraid to ask for help or advice.
10. Find extra strength from religious beliefs or political and moral ideals.

25

We have the technology

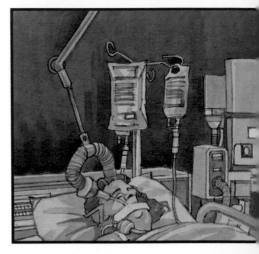

If a nurse from long ago could travel forward in time, she'd be amazed at how hospitals have changed. Today, nurses use the latest electronics to perform lifesaving tasks, from keeping patients' hearts beating to feeding tiny babies and delivering precise doses of powerful medicines and painkillers. Technology also monitors patients' vital signs and warns of sudden, risky changes. Modern medical machines are marvellous, but need skill and intelligence to operate. They are only as good as the expert nurses who work with them.

WIRED UP. Hopefully you will never need to be a patient in an intensive care unit. But if you were, you would find yourself hooked up to many machines. They would help keep you alive – even breathing for you, if necessary! And they would send the nurse minute-by-minute information about you.

How it works

High-tech medicine is VERY expensive. In the UK, it costs a hospital around £1,500 per day to treat someone in an intensive care unit.

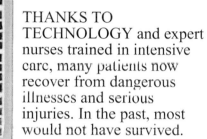

THANKS TO TECHNOLOGY and expert nurses trained in intensive care, many patients now recover from dangerous illnesses and serious injuries. In the past, most would not have survived.

Daring to care

Would you dare to face death and danger, if you didn't have to? Thousands of women did, in wartime. They volunteered to nurse wounded soldiers, mix medicines, wash bloody uniforms, make beds and roll bandages. They helped save lives, and their bravery won great respect and admiration. At first, volunteer war nurses were disorganised and untrained. But Florence Nightingale fought to send professional nurses to all British Army hospitals (she won, in 1866). And in 1901, the United States Army Nurse Corps was founded.

Ignore the guns - look after the patient!

SPECIAL SKILLS. Today's army, navy and airforce nurses are experts in emergency and critical care, operating theatre work, burns treatment and plastic surgery.

Modern army nurses are trained in fitness, discipline and combat as well as nursing skills. They have to work alongside fighting troops in very dangerous conditions.

NOT TOUGH ENOUGH? For centuries, army nurses were men. Officers said that women could not cope with battlefield conditions. The nurse volunteers proved them wrong!

COMPASSION AND COMFORT. Mary Seacole (1805–1881) travelled from Jamaica to Britain, then to the war zone in Crimea (Russia). She set up a meeting house for wounded British soldiers, gave them food and drink to warm them up, and mixed Caribbean herbal remedies to soothe their pain.

Care in the community

You never know when you might meet a nurse! Today, trained nurses don't just work in hospitals. They look after people in all kinds of different places – at work, on holiday, in offices, factories, airports, building sites, big shopping malls, community centres, film sets, sports stadiums and more. Nurses make home visits to people too old or too ill to visit a doctor, and run drop-in centres to treat minor illnesses and injuries. They also teach classes on healthy living, gentle exercise, baby care and first aid.

HELLO TO HEALTH. The first community nursing services began in England in 1859. Well-wishers paid for nurses to visit poor people in slum homes.

DIFFERENT OPPORTUNITIES. Nurses also sometimes work as researchers and sales people for pharmaceutical and cosmetics companies, or advise businesses, governments and the media.

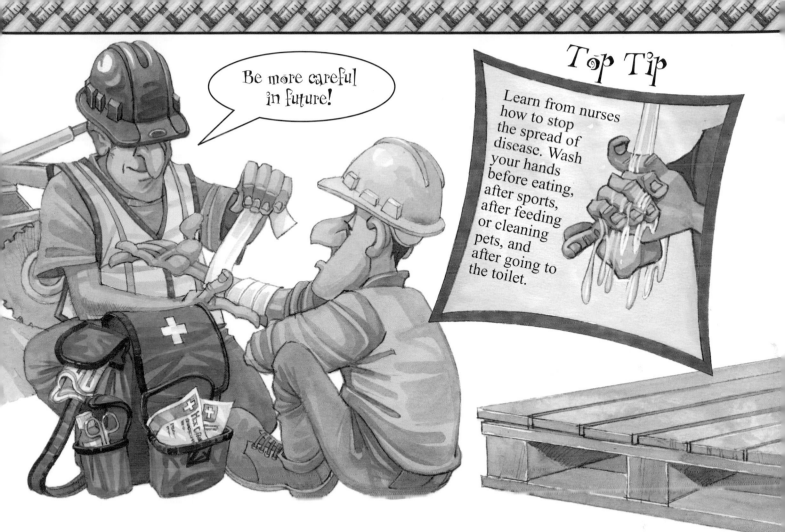

Learn from nurses how to stop the spread of disease. Wash your hands before eating, after sports, after feeding or cleaning pets, and after going to the toilet.

LEARN ALL ABOUT IT. Prevention is better than cure! Nurses give talks to young people, teaching them how to stay well and answering their health questions.

MOTHERS AND BABIES. Nurses with special training visit new mothers in their own homes, to check on the child's progress and the mother's well-being.

Nursing past, present and future

Nursing is one of the oldest careers, but it has changed a great deal over the centuries. And nurses today are still learning new skills and new techniques, based on the latest medical knowledge. They work as members of health care teams in hospitals and the community, to help save millions of lives. They also go to dangerous or disadvantaged places, to bring better health care to people living there. Whatever they do, and wherever they do it, we really wouldn't want to live without nurses!

This will soothe him!

PAST. At home or in hospital, nurses long ago kept patients comfortable, but often could not cure them.

You're making good progress!

PRESENT. Old-style caring skills are still important for nurses and their patients. But today's nurses also have many new duties.

Top tip

If you have health worries, visit the school nurse to make sure that you're doing all you can to keep yourself as healthy as possible.

FUTURE. Increasingly, nurses won't just care or cure – they will also work to prevent illness from happening.

SUPER-NURSES. Since 1971, highly trained nurse practitioners have taken over some of the tasks that doctors used to do. They have learned how to diagnose (identify) many common diseases and are licensed by governments to prescribe medicines to treat them.

Glossary

Amulet Lucky charm.

Anatomy Scientific study of the parts of the body.

Assess (a patient) Recognise what is wrong and decide on the best thing to do next.

Bacteria Tiny, single-celled organisms (living things) that are all around us. Some bacteria are helpful; others can cause diseases.

Commitment Being extremely devoted to a job (or a person).

Compassion Kindness, tenderness.

Competence Being skilful; doing a job well.

Diagnose Investigate a patient's symptoms and identify an illness or disease.

Hospice Peaceful, comforting care for patients who are dying; it can take place at home or in a hospice centre.

Humanitarian Helping and caring for humans in need.

Infect Pass on a disease.

Inhaler Medical device that delivers a measured dose of medicine into the body through the mouth.

Instinct Inborn feelings and behaviour.

Intensive care (also called **critical care**) Hospital rooms with special equipment and nursing staff to care for and monitor patients who are extremely ill.

Lice Tiny blood sucking insects that live on humans and other animals.

Pest house In the Middle Ages, a place where people with infectious diseases were locked away, so that they didn't infect others.

Physiology Scientific study of how the body works.

Plastic surgery Operation to change

a patient's appearance or to rebuild damaged parts of a patient's body.

Prescribe Select and give the best medicine to treat a patient's illness or relieve his or her suffering.

Professional A well-trained, respected person who is paid for his or her skills.

Quaker A member of the Society of Friends, a Christian-based religious movement that began in England in the 1650s. Quakers have worked for peace, tolerance, equality and social justice in many parts of the world.

Remedies Medicines or other substances designed to cure disease.

Stethoscope A medical device that helps doctors and nurses investigate a patient's heart, lungs, stomach and blood flow.

Surgery Medical treatment that involves operating on and/or cutting open the body.

Symptoms Changes (such as swelling or a rash) and/or pains in the body caused by disease. Each disease has its own special symptoms, though many symptoms can be caused by a variety of diseases.

Virus A tiny organism (living thing) that grows inside the cells of humans, animals and plants, and causes disease.

Vital signs Body functions, such as heart rate, blood pressure and temperature, that give important information about a patient's state of health or illness.

Index

Nursing heroes

There are a lot of nursing heroes in addition to the famous women you've just read about. Here is a list of some of them. You can do your own research to find out more.

Elizabeth Fry (1780–1845)
Inspired by her Quaker beliefs, Fry campaigned to reform prisons, help homeless people, and improve nursing care. In 1840, she set up a small nursing school in London. Later, some of her nurses worked with Florence Nightingale.

Mary Eliza Mahoney (1845–1926)
The daughter of freed slaves, Mahoney became the first African American to qualify as a trained nurse, in 1879. She was highly praised for her caring skills, and campaigned to abolish discrimination against nurses from minority communities.

Lillian Wald (1867–1940)
Wald was shocked by poverty and sickness in big cities. In 1893, in New York, she pioneered public health nursing. Wald's nurses not only cared for sick people but also offered free health checkups and advice on staying well, and worked to improve food, housing, education and welfare services.

Mary Breckenridge (1881–1965)
Breckenridge lived in the Kentucky countryside, far from doctors and nurses. After both her children died, she vowed to help other mothers and their families. She trained as a nurse and a midwife, and then, in 1925, set up the Frontier Nursing Service. It still trains and sends nurses to remote areas today.

Mother Teresa (1910–1997)
Born in present-day Macedonia, she became a nun, and then travelled to India to care for dying people in the slums. She devoted her life to 'the poorest of the poor' and recruited thousands of nurses to help her, in over 100 countries.

Hazel Johnson-Brown (1927–2011)
Brown had a brilliant career, serving as chief of the Army Nursing Corps, and then as a leader in modern nurse education. In 1979, she became the first African American woman to reach the rank of brigadier-general.

Did you know?

In opinion polls, nurses are regularly voted the 'most trusted professionals'.

On average, a hospital nurse walks at least 6 kilometres (4 miles) every day while caring for patients.

Hospitals are not always safe places to be. For example, American nurses report over 35,000 back injuries at work (mostly from lifting or moving patients) every year.

In 2010, researchers found that, on average, nurses washed their hands around 100 times during each 10-hour shift.

Japanese engineers have built robots to take over some of the simpler nursing duties, such as washing patients and carrying them to the bathroom.

In the United States and the UK, there are around four times as many nurses as doctors.

Worldwide, about one nurse in every ten is a man.

There are more than 20 million trained nurses working today, but they are not spread equally around the globe:

- In Africa, there are 805,000 nurses; that averages out to be 11 nurses for every 10,000 people.

- In North America and South America, there are 5,259,000 nurses; that is 61 nurses for every 10,000 people.

- In Europe, there are 6,620,000 nurses; that is 75 nurses for every 10,000 people.

Top tips on patient care

Over 2,000 years ago, ancient Greek doctors taught their male and female servants how to keep patients comfortable, even if they could not heal their injuries or cure their diseases. Their nursing advice was so helpful that trained nurses still follow many of these top tips to this day.

The ancient Greeks recommended:

- Clean, comfortable beds

- Lightweight, washable sheets and blankets

- Quiet, soothing surroundings

- Fresh air, but not too much of it

- Good, nourishing food, and water to drink

- Calm, undisturbed mealtimes

- Warm baths or massage to help ease pain

- Sweet-smelling oils and soft music to create a soothing, comforting atmosphere

- Gentle touch to comfort patients who are worried or afraid

- Plain, simple sickrooms—no bright lights, clashing patterns, or vivid colours